MW01110358

The Prophets of Hope Model

Catholic Education & Formation Ministries
328 West Kellogg Blvd.
St. Paul, MN 55102

Prophets of Hope

Profetas de Esperanza

❦ Prophets of Hope ❦

Volume 3

The Prophets of Hope Model

A Weekend Workshop

Prophets of Hope Editorial Team

Saint Mary's Press
Christian Brothers Publications
Winona, Minnesota

OF HOPE

WITNESSES

To young leaders, youth ministers, and pastoral agents who are giving their lives to carry Christ to Hispanic *jóvenes* in the United States.

Genuine recycled paper with 10% post-consumer waste.
Printed with soy-based ink.

The publishing team for this volume included Eduardo Arnouil, development editor; Jacqueline M. Captain, manuscript editor; Amy Schlumpf Manion, typesetter; Maurine R. Twait, art director; Jayne L. Stokke, cover designer; Alicia María Sánchez, illustrator; pre-press, printing, and binding by the graphics division of Saint Mary's Press.

Saint Mary's Press wishes to give special acknowledgement to the ACTA Foundation, for funding that helped to subsidize this publication.

The permissions are on page 67.

Copyright © 1997 by Saint Mary's Press, 702 Terrace Heights, Winona, MN 55987-1320. All rights reserved. Permission is granted to reproduce only the materials intended for distribution to the workshop participants. No other part of this book may be reproduced by any means without the written permission of the publisher.

Printed in the United States of America

Printing: 9 8 7 6 5 4 3 2 1

Year: 2005 04 03 02 01 00 99 98 97

ISBN 0-88489-451-7

Library of Congress Catalog Card Number: 96-71261

Prophets of Hope Editorial Team

Writers:	Eduardo Arnouil
	Carmen María Cervantes, EdD
Consultants:	Alejandro Aguilera-Titus
	Carlos Carrillo
	Juan Díaz-Vilar, SJ
	Dolores Díez-de-Sollano, SH
	Rev. Juan J. Huitrado-Rizo
	Antonio Medina-Rivera, PhD
Translators into English:	Robert Brancatelli
	José María Matty-Cervantes
Secretaries:	Aurora Macías-Dewhirst
	José María Matty-Cervantes

❧ Contents ❧

The Prophets of Hope Model: A Weekend Workshop is the third volume in the Prophets of Hope series. Its goal is to help pastoral agents and adult leaders experience and understand the vision, methodology, and pastoral principles of the Prophets of Hope model for missionary and evangelizing communities of young adults. To achieve its goal, this book offers the necessary elements to hold a weekend workshop for a region, diocese, or parish. For best results, the workshop should be done with thirty to fifty people so that up to five small communities can be formed.

In this book, as in the entire Witnesses of Hope collection, the terms *joven, jóvenes,* and *juventud* may be used occasionally to refer to people in the age span from sixteen to twenty-four years old because there is no equivalent concept in the English language for this sociological group. A young person, male or female, aged sixteen to twenty-four is called a *joven* if he or she is single. *Jóvenes* is the plural of *joven. Juventud* refers to the sociological group formed by *jóvenes.* As with the other resources that Saint Mary's Press is publishing for the Prophets of Hope model, this book is aimed at people age sixteen and older. If there is a need to use this material with younger teenagers, it should be adapted.

The book is divided into three parts. The first part contains instructions for planning and implementing the workshop. The second part presents the process to be used for the weekend workshop. The third part contains four documents that can help in learning the Prophets of Hope model and four resources that serve as practical tools for the process of the workshop.

The Prophets of Hope Model is designed especially for young adult ministers and leaders who are planning and conducting the workshop. Young adults participating in the workshop may also use it for reflection, recording their experiences, and planning liturgies. Therefore, it is recommended that each member of the coordination team and every participant have their own copy. In this way the formation experience is accessible to more people, and everyone can learn how to give the workshops.

The Prophets of Hope process

Prophets of Hope was chosen as the name of the model because of the hope small communities offer Hispanic *jóvenes,* the Catholic church, and society in general. This model begins with the experience of Hispanic *jóvenes* in the United States, and shares in the theological and pastoral vision and spirituality of Hispanic young adult ministry outlined at the three Encuentros Nacionales de Pastoral Hispana. It also adopts the general objective of the National Pastoral Plan for Hispanic Ministry, which is intended to help Latino *jóvenes* do the following:

> To live and promote by means of a *Pastoral de Conjunto,* a model of church that is: communitarian, evangelizing, and missionary; incarnate in the reality of the Hispanic people and open to the diversity of cultures; a promoter and example of justice; active in developing leadership through integral education; leaven for the Kingdom of God in society. (National Conference of Catholic Bishops, *National Pastoral Plan for Hispanic Ministry,* p. 8)

The goal of the Prophets of Hope model is to promote the Christian formation and life of young adults through their participation in small communities. This model fosters a close relationship between the faith and life of young adults, bringing the Gospel into the affective, intellectual, spiritual, and sociopolitical dimensions of their life. It furthers the spirit of evangelization, community, and mission promoted in the New Evangelization called for by Pope John Paul II. It comes from a prophetic perspective and leads to the empowerment of young adults so that they might overcome the obstacles that prevent them from living in loving communion with God and one another.

To become more familiar with this model, please study the illustration and description of the Prophets of Hope process in document 1 on page 40. You should also review document 4 on the Witnesses of Hope collection, found on pages 52–53. This collection is being published as a resource for implementing the model. For a more complete overview of the model, please read the entire Witnesses of Hope collection. For training and assistance in the implementation of the model, please contact Instituto Fe y Vida, 1737 West Benjamin Holt Drive, Stockton, CA 95207-3422.

The editorial staff would like to hear from you with your evaluation of the process, any adaptations you make, and your recommendations for future reference. Please write to us at *Proyecto de Pastoral Juvenil Hispana,* 1737 West Benjamin Holt Drive, Stockton, CA 95207-3422.

PART 1

Instructions for Using This Book

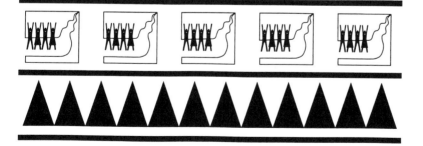

Overview

To meet the objective of this book—experiencing and understanding the vision, methodology, and pastoral principles of the Prophets of Hope model—the workshop must be prepared and implemented in a spirit of community. Preparation of the workshop constitutes a formation-in-action experience. Therefore it is important for all participants to get involved in some kind of ministry. Toward this end, the preparation is done in two stages: long-term preparation with the formation of a coordination team, and immediate preparation with the formation of seven service teams.

Long-term preparation and formation of the coordination team

Long-term preparation begins with the formation of a coordination team consisting of approximately twelve persons. With the exception of the small-community advisers, who are pastoral agents or persons with pastoral experience who can function during the workshop as advisers of the small communities, the rest of the coordination team should be made up of *jóvenes*.

Each of the five small communities needs an adviser, and each of the seven service teams needs a coordinator. If the workshop is regional, individuals from the different dioceses should form the coordination team. If the workshop is for a diocese, persons from different parishes should make up the team. If the workshop is for only one parish, care should be taken to include representatives from each of the different groups attending the workshop.

The coordination team should set aside a full day to plan the workshop. Ideally this planning meeting is held four months before the workshop, allowing enough time for publicity and adequate preparation. Registration of participants should begin at least two weeks prior to the workshop date.

During the long-term preparation, the coordination team has the following duties:

1. **Contract the site for the workshop.** The workshop can be held at either a retreat house or a similar site.

2. **Plan the workshop.** Planning for the workshop will include setting the planning calendar, reviewing the workshop's program on pages 17–18, adjusting the schedule to the time available, and adapting the process as necessary.

3. **Assign responsibilities for the different sessions.** The coordination team should choose individuals who will be responsible for the general introduction to the workshop and the workshop's process. The presentation of the Prophets of Hope model on page 31, in session 4, should be given by someone who has worked with the model and knows it well.

4. **Assign a community adviser for each of the five small communities.** The advisers should become familiar with the roles the community members will participate in so that they can help when needed. These roles appear in document 2, "Roles in the Small Communities of *Jóvenes*," on pages 43–45. The advisers should have prior experience with small communities, or with the formation process for implementing the Prophets of Hope model. Small communities form in the first session of the workshop. With the exception of the advisers, who are assigned beforehand, members of each community elect their own facilitator, timekeeper, and secretary.

5. **Form and coordinate the service teams.** The teams and their responsibilities are described in the next section.

Immediate preparation and formation of the service teams

During the immediate preparation, the coordination team must ensure that all those participating in the workshop have some role in its preparation and implementation so that they will get to know one another better and will foster a communitarian spirit. Seven service teams work best. If necessary, individuals may be allowed to serve on two different teams.

To begin the team formation process, hold a three-hour meeting two weeks before the workshop. The objective of this meeting is for all workshop participants to sign up, according to their gifts, for the team or teams they wish to serve on. If participants come from distant geographic areas, each area can be responsible for a different ministry. In these cases, the preparation meeting can be held at the discretion of the team coordinators.

Here is a list of the service teams and their functions:

The hospitality team is in charge of registration and on-site orientation. This team is also responsible for welcoming the workshop participants, arranging for food, and preparing a medical or first-aid kit.

The logistics team is made up of at least ten people who are responsible for preparing the meeting rooms before the workshop, maintaining them during the workshop, and cleaning them afterward. In addition, team members make sure that all activities are done within the allotted time. To ensure the smooth flow of activities, two timekeepers are assigned to each segment of the workshop: Friday night; Saturday morning, afternoon, and evening; and Sunday morning and afternoon.

The pep and warm-up team is composed of two or three people in charge of the opening icebreaker (and similar exercises throughout the workshop), games, and social activities. This team's role is to encourage participants to interact while helping them have a pleasant and enriching weekend. This team works in conjunction with the music team.

The liturgy team is responsible for prayers, liturgies, and the liturgical environment. This team works in conjunction with the music team.

The music team selects, rehearses, and directs the songs for each day, and supplies songbooks for all the participants. This team works closely with the liturgy team and the pep and warm-up team.

The secretarial team consists of two persons responsible for writing the minutes of the preparatory meetings, collecting material produced from the workshop, and identifying individuals to write articles about their experiences in the workshop for publication in parish bulletins or diocesan newspapers.

The evaluation team is responsible for preparing either an oral or a written evaluation of the workshop, analyzing it, and making recommendations for improvement.

**Time Frame for the Implementation
of the Prophets of Hope Workshop**

- Planning Meeting . . . . 4 months before
  (Coordination team) . . . . the workshop

- Service Team Coordinating Meeting . . . . 2 weeks before
  (Coordination team and all participants) . . . . the workshop

- Workshop

Follow-up Possibilities

Option A → Repeat the weekend workshop somewhere else.

Option B → Begin with the creation of small communities, guided by Agents of Hope, manual 1: *Dawn on the Horizon.*

During the implementation of the workshop

The coordination, music, logistics, and hospitality teams should arrive early on the day of the workshop to welcome the participants, prepare the meeting rooms, and set up the music. As participants arrive, those who are not already on a service team are assigned to one. If need be, the coordination team may meet during the evenings of the workshop for twenty minutes to discuss the activities of the following day.

Methodology

In order for the workshop participants to experience and understand the vision, methodology, and pastoral principles of the Prophets of Hope model, they will follow the "pastoral circle": *being— seeing—judging—acting—evaluating—celebrating,* as explained in document 3, "The Pastoral Circle According to the Prophets of Hope Model," on pages 46–51. Each one of the steps in the pastoral circle is developed in the workshop sessions. Below is a brief explanation of what these steps are, and how they can be implemented in the workshop.

Being

The first workshop session emphasizes the individuality of each participant when forming communities. The rest of the sessions are done in small communities, allowing participants to experience the communitarian model. During the workshop, participants will be able to understand what makes up their growth as persons, and to see how small communities develop into cells within an evangelizing and missionary church.

Seeing

In this session the participants will analyze their reality through an exercise that introduces them to the five dimensions of young people's lives, as covered by the Prophets of Hope model. The five dimensions of young people's lives are their process of maturation, their human relationships, their culture, their role in social transformation, and their religious reality.

Judging

In this session the participants will use a reflection based on a passage of the Scriptures and a quote from an ecclesial document to judge their reality in light of the Gospel and the teachings of the church. The texts have been selected to help the participants become aware of the five stages of their development as laypeople, according to the Prophets of Hope model. These stages are the Covenant with God, the following of Jesus, the action in history, the commitment as church, and the building of a new culture and society.

Acting

The participants experience a formation-in-action process throughout the weekend. In addition, the fourth session of the workshop helps the participants envision Christian praxis in community and draft a plan for using the Prophets of Hope model to improve their ministry.

Evaluating

Several times during the workshop the coordination team will be able to evaluate different aspects of the workshop through observation of, and dialog with, the participants. In addition, in the last session the participants will evaluate their weekend experience, will become aware of its contributions and challenges, and will offer constructive criticism to improve this type of workshop.

Celebrating

In this workshop, the participants will celebrate life through gatherings, songs, and group games and dynamics. They will also learn how to integrate life and the celebration of their faith through prayer and by creating a closing liturgy based on their experience of the weekend.

Workshop program

This section is a detailed program for the weekend. The process for the workshop, developed in part 2, contains only the process and content necessary to meet the book's objective. Group dynamics, games, songs, and some of the prayers are left to the creative imagination of the participants.

In the Prophets of Hope model the tasks of organization, reflection, and prayer are an essential part of the process for all participants. The commentaries offered in this book are designed so that local communities become the authors of their communal experience during this weekend and beyond.

Friday

Welcome and icebreaker (30 minutes)

General introduction (30 minutes)

Opening prayer (30 minutes)

Session 1: We are people in community [being] (1 hour, 30 minutes)
A. Forming small communities
B. Reflecting on personal talents, gifts, and charisms
C. Discerning gifts
D. Communal prayer: Send us your gifts, Lord! (45 minutes)
E. Social

Saturday

Morning prayer and introduction to the day (30 minutes)

Session 2: Integrating the small communities in relation to the five dimensions of reality [seeing] (3 hours, 15 minutes)
A. Presenting the five dimensions and assigning topics
B. A closer look at the five dimensions of reality
C. Preparing the first part of the banner
D. Large-group meeting

Session 3: Life in light of our Christian vocation and mission [judging] (3 hours, 45 minutes)
A. The five stages of Christian formation
B. Personal reflection
C. Creating the second part of the banner
D. Liturgy preparation
E. Liturgy of the word: Acting through history with God (2 hours)
F. Social

Sunday

Morning prayer and introduction to the day (30 minutes)

Session 4: Preparing for an evangelizing action [acting] (3 hours, 30 minutes)
A. Introduction
B. Reflecting on our pastoral action
C. Presentation of the Prophets of Hope model
D. Open forum on the Prophets of Hope model
E. Pastoral action planning

Session 5: The Eucharist, the rite of commitment, and sending forth [celebrating] (2 hours)
A. Introduction
B. Preparation
C. Eucharist

Session 6: Workshop evaluation [evaluating] (30 minutes)
A. Written evaluation
B. Oral evaluation

PART 2

Process for the
Weekend Workshop

Introduction to the weekend workshop process

Through this workshop, participants will experience key aspects of the Prophets of Hope model. The objectives for the participants of the workshop are as follows:

- to become familiar with the pastoral-theological foundations behind the model and the phases of the process needed for its implementation
- to learn about the model's holistic approach and the maturation process it fosters
- to experience the nature of a communitarian pastoral ministry
- to become aware of the need for an evangelizing and missionary ministry
- to practice the pastoral circle that the Prophets of Hope model uses as its methodological approach: *being—seeing—judging—acting—evaluating—celebrating*
- to reflect on the implementation of the model and to make an initial plan for its implementation

The workshop hopes to achieve these objectives by offering participants an experience of each of the six phases of the pastoral circle within a communitarian pastoral focus. At the same time, it presents the key aspects of the pastoral-theological foundations of the Prophets of Hope model.

Session 1
We are people in community: Being

Objectives

- to form the communities in which the participants will work during the weekend
- to reflect on the participants' personal gifts and identify the *jóvenes* who will serve the small community as group facilitators, secretaries, and timekeepers
- to experience the Prophets of Hope model in small communities

Procedure

A. Forming small communities

The small communities should be formed by means of a game or group dynamic. During this weekend each community should have from eight to twelve members so that all the roles are fulfilled, yet everyone has an opportunity to participate.

In real life, the small communities should have anywhere from twelve to twenty-four members. *Dawn on the Horizon,* manual 1 in the Agents of Hope series, contains a process designed especially for the formation of small communities. It also provides participants with a six-month experience in an evangelizing and pastoral ministry in small communities.

The experience of *being* a person in an evangelizing community and in a community of communities starts here. This experience is lived during the whole workshop.

B. Reflecting on personal talents, gifts, and charisms

1. Each community prays to God for the ability to recognize the personal gifts and qualities each member can offer for the good of the community.

2. Each participant fills in resource 1, "Personal Gifts for Serving the Community," which can be found on page 54.

C. Discerning gifts

1. Each person shares his or her total score from resource 1, "Personal Gifts for Serving the Community." One person jots down all the scores for the community. The five participants with the highest overall scores are identified.

2. The roles needed by the community are read out loud. They are secretarial, group facilitation, and timekeeping. These roles appear in document 2 "Roles in the Small Communities of *Jóvenes*" on pages 43–45. Due to the short duration of this workshop, the role of coordinator is assumed by the coordinating team and there is not enough time to select an *animador/a*.

3. The five participants with the highest overall scores reflect on the nature of the roles. They then share with the community the roles they feel most qualified to fill. If two or more are inclined to-

ward the same role, the community asks questions to help them reach the best decision.

4. Each community reports the results of its discernment to the whole group. The persons chosen serve their communities for the remainder of the workshop.

The discernment process just described is appropriate only for a weekend workshop or similar event. In reality, the discernment process should be more in depth, especially in relation to the *animadores* and the coordinators.

D. Communal prayer: Send us your gifts, Lord!

Long-term preparation. The liturgy team should obtain a sufficient quantity of small plastic cups, so that each participant, including the coordination team, gets one. There should be ten plastic cups left over. Each cup should be labeled with a quality or gift the community needs. For instance, the label might have any one of the following: happiness, forgiveness, willingness to listen, perseverance, patience, solidarity, commitment, or authenticity.

Short-term preparation. A small altar, with the labeled plastic cups on it, is placed in the center of the meeting room. If desired, the altar can be placed to the side and left there for the duration of the workshop. Participants may pray there for a particular quality or gift they might need.

1. A member of the liturgy team invites the participants to experience the presence of God

2. A member of the liturgy team asks someone to read 1 Corinthians 12:1–11.

3. Invite the participants to select from the altar a cup labeled with a quality or gift that can help them get more involved in the church community. The participants take the cups back with them to where they were sitting.

4. Allow several minutes of silence to follow so that each person can reflect on the gift he or she is asking for.

5. Ask the participants to share their reflections in groups of six to eight people. Afterward they create a prayer that incorporates all the reflections. They then choose a person to recite the prayer aloud.

6. Have everyone form a circle around the altar. The designated persons recite the prayers out loud. Meanwhile the rest of the members in their small group put the cups back on the altar.

7. Close with a song.

E. Social

Session 2
Integrating the small communities in relation to the five dimensions of reality: Seeing

Objectives

- to look at the reality of *jóvenes* from five different dimensions—the process of maturation, human relationships, culture, social transformation, and religious reality
- to integrate *jóvenes* into the community and then choose a name and symbol to represent the community

Advance preparation. During this and the following session, each community prepares a banner with magazine clippings and drawings. Items needed include newsprint (six feet per community), magazines, scissors, glue, and markers.

Procedure

A. Presenting the five dimensions and assigning topics

The person responsible for this session does an introduction on the five dimensions of the reality of young adults mentioned in the objective. Then she or he assigns a dimension to each community and gives instructions on how to conduct the community reflection.

The first five chapters in volume 1 of the Prophets of Hope series, *Hispanic Young People and the Church's Pastoral Response,* may be used as a resource. The presentation should be brief, but it should furnish reasons for the five dimensions and show key aspects of each.

The experience of *seeing* the reality in which the participants live is emphasized in this session. This experience informs the rest of the workshop.

B. A closer look at the five dimensions of reality

1. For their reflection on the different aspects of the assigned dimensions, the small communities may use resource 2, "Reflections on the Five Dimensions of Reality," on pages 55–59, which contains some information on each of the dimensions. Enough time should be allowed for each small community to read the paragraph describing its dimension, to add anything important that is not covered on the resource, and to answer the questions.

2. Each small community forms two groups. One group brainstorms the gifts and qualities of *jóvenes* in relation to the assigned dimension, the other group brainstorms the challenges. Each group then identifies the five most important gifts and qualities, or its five biggest challenges.

3. The two groups meet to share their results.

4. The entire small community identifies concrete ways to use its gifts to overcome its challenges. These are written down.

C. Preparing the first part of the banner

In this exercise, the participants work on a small-community banner and come up with a name and symbol for their small community.

1. The materials for the banner are distributed. Small-community members find and cut out illustrations depicting the gifts and challenges they identified in their reflection.

2. Small-community members take turns explaining why they chose particular illustrations for their banner. Then, based on this discussion, they create together the name and symbol that will represent their small community.

3. Small-community members decide how to assemble their banner so that the small community's name, symbol, and members' illustrations all fit.

D. Large-group meeting

Each small community presents its banner to the whole group and explains why it chose this name and symbol.

Session 3
Life in light of our Christian vocation and mission: Judging

Objectives

- to judge reality in light of the five stages of Christian formation and life
- to experience the relationship between personal faith life and community life

Procedure

This step can be done in two ways depending on the level of pastoral experience of the participants. If they are in an initial stage of faith formation, the small-community members should read and reflect on Matthew 13:31–32. If they are more advanced, they can proceed with the exercise as presented below.

A. The five stages of Christian formation

The person in charge explains how participants will experience the *judging* step of the pastoral circle by reflecting on reality in light of the Scriptures and church documents. He or she then assigns one of the five stages of Christian formation and life from the Prophets of Hope model to each small community. This should be done according to the dimension of reality each small community worked on in session 2. The stages may be assigned in the following way:

Dimensions of Reality	*Themes for Reflection*
Process of maturation	In Covenant with God
Human relationships	Followers of Jesus
Social transformation	Acting through history
Religious reality	Committed as church
Culture	Fostering culture and society

B. Personal reflection

This reflection is based on resource 3, "Themes for a Reflection on Christian Faith and Life," pages 60–64. An explanation of how to do the reflection should take place before the participants start. This reflection should be done in silence. If possible, small-community members may go outside to a garden or chapel.

C. Creating the second part of the banner

1. Each small community meets, and members share one important aspect of their personal reflection. The secretary takes notes.

2. The members review the notes, identifying similar or complementary comments. Then they summarize the message of their personal reflections in five words or phrases.

3. Keeping the five key words or phrases in mind, the small community asks itself the following question: What does God ask us to do in our daily life, in our parish, and in our neighborhood? Responses are written on the banner.

D. Liturgy preparation

1. A member of the liturgy team introduces the theme of the liturgy, leads a short reflection summarizing the workshop experience thus far, and then explains how the preparation will be done. Below are ideas that may be used for the introduction, and questions that may help in summarizing the workshop experience.

God becomes manifest through events in life and prayer. Jesus saw his Father acting in history just as Jesus himself acted in order for his followers to experience the loving and liberating presence of God. As followers of Jesus, we have the same task before us today: to act in such a way that the stories of individuals and peoples become part of the story of salvation. In this way we become coauthors with Jesus in the mission of building the Reign of God in the world.

In these two days we have reflected on different aspects of life and the Gospel to discover the presence of God among us. God called us in an explicit way to be coworkers with him from the moment of our baptism. At our baptism we were clothed with Christ and became God's children and the brothers and sisters of Jesus and all humanity. This was the experience Jesus had at his own baptism, when he discovered he was the Beloved Son and Chosen One of God. After his discovery Jesus prepared for the mission of proclaiming forgiveness of sins, liberation from oppression, healing of the sick, and granting of new life to those who followed him.

In this liturgy we want to make Jesus present among *jóvenes* with whom we live. But before doing so we need to dwell on the experience of this workshop to help us prepare. The following questions may help:

- How have the reflections and exercises enabled us to hear God's call to change the world?
- How can *jóvenes* help write a story that fulfills God's desires for themselves, all Hispanic people, and the United States?
- What are the greatest obstacles to writing a story in accordance with God's plan for humanity?

2. Each small community prepares a skit symbolizing Jesus acting in youth ministry, based on one of the following passages from the Gospel of Mark. The scene should depict the events in the passage as if they were occurring today.
- The calling of the Twelve: 3:13–19; 6:7–13
- The parable of the sower: 4:3–20
- The multiplication of loaves: 6:35–44
- The rich young man: 10:17–22
- The Last Supper: 14:12–25

3. Each small community chooses an object that symbolizes the work it has done during the workshop and presents the object in the liturgy. Banners may not be used at this time because they will be part of the closing liturgy.

E. Liturgy of the word: Acting through history with God

Entrance song

Rite of reconciliation. Small-community members are encouraged to ask for forgiveness for acts of omission in which they failed to make the Reign of God present around them. The following are examples of petitions for forgiveness: We ask your forgiveness for not having attended to the sick; or We ask your forgiveness for the times when our gossip led to division.

All respond: *Lord, have mercy on us.*

Psalm: We bless you and place our trust in you. Each small community reads the stanza corresponding to its reflection theme, and everyone responds with the responsorial psalm.

All:
We bless you and place our trust in you, God our Father, through your only Son, our Lord Jesus Christ.

Community:
When the day is done and we approach night,
blessed for the light in our life and thankful
for the chance to *live in Covenant with you*
and our brothers and sisters,
full of joy we sing of our desire
to be your people and to live our Covenant
with fidelity.

All:
We bless you and place our trust in you, God our Father,
through your only Son, our Lord Jesus Christ.

Community:
In love you sent to us your Divine Son
so that he may bring us your love, justice, and peace.
Through him you renewed and continue to renew
the hope of new life to all who follow Jesus.
Help us to be *followers of Jesus,*
working hard to build the Reign of God,
with *jóvenes* who need it most.

All:
We bless you and place our trust in you, God our Father,
through your only Son, our Lord Jesus Christ.

Community:
Thank you for this day filled with your presence.
We worship you for the joy of being together,
for the efforts we have made during this workshop,
for our work in communities,
and for granting us opportunities to pray.
We know that in these ways we are *acting through history,*
shaping it according to your heart's desires.

All:
We bless you and place our trust in you, God our Father,
through your only Son, our Lord Jesus Christ.

Community:
We have listened to your word of life
and remembered the grace of our baptism.
We open our heart and communities
so that you become our teacher and Lord.
We renew *our commitment as church,*
to be signs and instruments of your love,
first to those who need it most.

All:
We bless you and place our trust in you, God our Father,
through your only Son, our Lord Jesus Christ.

Community:
Just as you overlook our faults and laziness,
paying attention to our good works,
just as dawn emerges from night,
help us to *foster a culture and a society*
led by the values Jesus taught us.

All:
We bless you and place our trust in you, God our Father,
through your only Son, our Lord Jesus Christ.

Gospel reading. Each small community reads its scriptural passage and performs its drama, at the end of which a community member says, "This is the Word of God, incarnate today among *jóvenes* with whom we live." After the communities have all read their scriptural passage and performed their dramas, all respond: "Thanks be to God."

Offering. One person from each small community presents the object that symbolizes the community's work, and explains its meaning.

Closing song. The participants sing the selected song while standing in a circle arm-in-arm and swaying. The closing song should reflect the unity of all communities touched by the same Spirit.

F. Social

Session 4

Preparing for an evangelizing action: Acting

Objectives

- to discern the general goal and specific objectives of the pastoral ministry among *jóvenes* communities
- to identify concrete pastoral actions in light of the workshop

Procedure

A. Introduction

The person in charge of this session gives a short introduction and explains how it will be conducted. It is important to emphasize that in the workshop, the dimension of acting happens according to the pastoral circle, which is a formation-in-action process. However, the real acting takes place in daily life. Because this session involves initial pastoral planning, it is advisable to form groups by diocese or parish, depending on whether the workshop is regional or diocesan.

B. Reflecting on our pastoral action

1. A member of the coordination team invites the participants to form groups by diocese or parish.

2. The participants are invited to study, in silence, the small-community practices described in resource 4, "Praxis of a Community of Disciples of Jesus," on pages 65–66. Each group member ranks the practices in order of importance, placing first those she or he needs to work on most, either with the current youth group or with a future small community.

3. Each group chooses a facilitator, a secretary, and a timekeeper for the discussion.

4. Each group member shares what he or she believes are the three most important practices. The secretary notes these on newsprint.

5. Each small group reviews its notes and moves toward consensus.

6. Each small group identifies the three most important activities for the group, discusses them for fifteen minutes, and includes reasons for picking these three.

C. Presentation of the Prophets of Hope model

The person making this presentation should know the Prophets of Hope model and process well enough to highlight the most relevant parts for the workshop participants and to answer their questions. A review of the first two volumes in the Prophets of Hope series, *Hispanic Young People and the Church's Pastoral Response* and *Evangelization of Hispanic Young People,* would be helpful.

The first volume analyzes the five dimensions of reality for young people mentioned in resource 2, "Reflections on the Five Dimensions of Reality," on pages 55–59. It also talks about the evangelizing mission of the church, and small young adult communities as a model for pastoral action. The second volume addresses evangelization in each of the following dimensions: Jesus as prophet of the Reign of God; the evangelizing action of God, the evangelizers, and the evangelized; Prophets of Hope as a community model of evangelization; and Mary as pilgrim of faith, prophet of hope, and model for an evangelizing practice. All of these are essential aspects of the Prophets of Hope model.

In addition, it would be helpful to review manual 1 of the Agents of Hope series, *Dawn on the Horizon: Creating Small Communities.* This manual offers the opportunity to achieve a deeper understanding of ministry in evangelizing and missionary small communities. It also provides an appropriate process for creating small communities, and the opportunity to experience life in a small community for a six-month period.

A more systematic presentation of the Prophets of Hope process appears in document 1, on pages 40–42, which contains an illustration and a brief description of its process. Document 4 on pages 52–53 is a chart of the Witnesses of Hope collection and may be used as a visual resource to further clarify the model.

D. Open forum on the Prophets of Hope model

The objective of this forum is to address any doubts or concerns participants may have about the model and its implementation. Some of the questions may be related to the way their parish functions and the concept of young adult ministry it holds.

Therefore, the following considerations should be taken into account:

- Pastoral ministry among young people in the United States usually consists of youth ministry for high-school-aged youth, and young adult ministry for those eighteen and older. Frequently, Hispanic ministry among *jóvenes* is done with persons eighteen and older. When this happens, Hispanic ministry among *jóvenes* should be treated like young adult ministry and should be organized according to models for adults.

- More and more parishes in the United States are turning to the small community model of ministry. These communities often go by various names, such as faith-sharing communities, Christian communities, or, simply, small communities. The Prophets of Hope model has been designed especially for the pastoral needs of small communites of *jóvenes* in the United States, and for the purpose of promoting pastoral action in the church and the world.

- The small communities follow an evangelical model of ecclesial organization and pastoral ministry, which works well with the Latino culture, where the extended family and the experience of community are very important.

- It is important that the small ecclesial communities maintain a spirit of communion with the rest of the church, and a close relationship with the parish and diocese. This does not mean the small community has to meet at the parish center. Christian faithful have the right and obligation to seek out the most suitable ways of organizing with the purpose of pursuing faith formation. They also should seek out the support they need to live according to the Gospel and to bring their pastoral ministry to life.

- One advantage of the Prophets of Hope model is that it has support material in both English and Spanish. This means small communities of *jóvenes* can come together in either language. The books have been designed to help ethnic groups and immigrant people interact among themselves and with one another. Thus the parish can count on a variety of small young adult communities, which taken together make up one great community of communities.

E. Pastoral action planning

The whole group discusses pastoral action planning by answering the following questions. The secretary records the conclusions drawn from this exercise on newsprint. The newsprint should have a clear heading containing the name of each diocese or parish and of the subject being discussed. Then the secretary summarizes the conclusions for the group. The notes will serve as a starting point for future meetings, and as source material for an article in the parish bulletin or diocesan newspaper.

1. In light of your experience and from the reflections, what *actions* can be taken to improve your ministry? Make a list.

2. Would repeating this workshop with other *jóvenes* be worthwhile? Why? When? What help would you need with the preparation? Put your conclusions in writing.

3. Are you interested in organizing yourselves in small communities? If yes, what help will you need? Put your ideas in writing.

4. Conduct a large-group meeting and have each group briefly share its conclusions.

Session 5
The Eucharist, the rite of commitment, and sending forth: Celebrating

A. Introduction
The objective of this introduction is to inspire the preparation of the eucharistic celebration.

The Eucharist is the celebration *par excellence* of the ecclesial community. During this weekend we have made a conscious effort to relate to one another as small communities, thereby forming one community of communities. The Eucharist, therefore, is the most appropriate way of closing this workshop. In addition, the Eucharist is the sacrament of thanksgiving for God's action in human history, for the new and eternal Covenant we have through Jesus Christ, and for the transformation of our personal stories into the story of salvation.

Linked to the sacrifice of Jesus, we use the profession of faith in the Eucharist to prepare ourselves to offer our life and work to God. As a true faith community, we call upon the Holy Spirit to transform bread and wine into the body and blood of Christ so that, assembled as one, we will be fortified and filled with the Holy Spirit as one body and spirit in Christ.

We hope to leave this workshop as one community of men and women who, filled with the Holy Spirit, are committed to the evangelization of others. We also hope that our final amen may reflect our faith and commitment to be coworkers in the saving work of Jesus.

The Eucharist is an experience that lasts throughout one's life. Our celebration today is a thanksgiving for the blessings of God, and a way to become more authentic disciples of Christ. Through the Eucharist we will let the Holy Spirit give meaning to our life. With this in mind, we should prepare the petitions, asking God for this eucharistic dimension in our life.

The following list presents different ways to live out our communion with Christ as church. This list can be used for the petitions.

- talking personally to God and the community
- recognizing and proclaiming the greatness of God without asking for anything in return
- thanking God for the salvation offered to us freely through Jesus Christ
- offering ourselves to God, together with Jesus, personally and through the community
- living out our salvation through the reconciliation and union offered to us through our Covenant with God
- opening ourselves so that the Holy Spirit fills our heart, transforms us, and gives us new life
- being open to the love of God and responding to that love
- giving ourselves over to Christ so that we recognize our solidarity with those who are suffering
- encouraging a sense of the universal church with one faith and one Spirit but a diversity of forms
- being a pilgrim church, acting in human events, and bringing about the Reign of God through the Spirit

B. Preparation

Since this is a Sunday Mass, the readings must come from the Sunday lectionary. If the readings are judged inappropriate for the occasion, ask the priest if substitutions may be made.

Some participants may want to receive the sacrament of reconciliation before the eucharistic celebration. The priest should allow enough time for this.

Because the theme of the eucharistic celebration will vary from workshop to workshop, two general recommendations are offered here for planning the liturgy:

Capture the experience of the workshop. This can be done with symbols or by using the banners in the entrance rite, as an altar cloth, or as a decoration in the offertory. Also there are moments in the liturgy that can relate specifically to the workshop, such as the rite of reconciliation, the homily (which can be a dialog), prayers of the faithful, and thanksgiving after communion.

Include a rite of commitment and sending forth. After the Eucharist, the presider may conduct a rite in which participants renew their commitment to Jesus Christ by deepening their faith, by becoming missionaries who spread the Reign of God, and by bringing other *jóvenes* to Jesus.

C. Eucharist
- Entrance song
- Rite of reconciliation
- First reading
- Psalm
- Second reading
- Alleluia
- Gospel
- Homily
- Petitions
- Preparation of gifts
- Consecration
- Lord's Prayer
- Sign of peace
- Communion song
- Thanksgiving
- Rite of commitment and sending forth

Session 6
Workshop evaluation: Evaluating

In order to allow the Eucharist to crown the experience as a community of communities, the *celebrating* aspect of the pastoral circle is inverted in this workshop in relation to its place in the pastoral circle. In the ongoing formation process of the Prophets of Hope model, the evaluation is done in meetings dedicated to it, followed by a social outing.

The following evaluation form can be photocopied for distribution and analysis.

A. Written evaluation

Workshop evaluation on *The Prophets of Hope Model*
Please rate the workshop sessions and the workshop in general using a scale from 1 to 5, with 1 representing poor and 5 representing excellent. Please circle the number and then write in any comments.

Evaluation of the sessions
Session 1: We are people in community *[being]*

                     1   2   3   4   5

    Comments:

Session 2: Integrating the small communities
in relation to the five dimensions of reality *[seeing]*

                     1   2   3   4   5

    Comments:

Session 3: Life in light of our Christian vocation and mission
[judging]

                     1   2   3   4   5

    Comments:

Session 4: Preparing for an evangelizing action *[acting]*

        1   2   3   4   5

Comments:

Session 5: The Eucharist, the rite of commitment,
and sending forth *[celebrating]*

        1   2   3   4   5

Comments:

General evaluation

• Coordination

        1   2   3   4   5

Comments:

• Publicity

        1   2   3   4   5

Comments:

• Hospitality

        1   2   3   4   5

Comments:

• Pep and warm-up

        1   2   3   4   5

Comments:

• Advisers

        1   2   3   4   5

Comments:

• Use of time

                  1   2   3   4   5

    Comments:

• Site

                  1   2   3   4   5

    Comments:

• Meals

                  1   2   3   4   5

    Comments:

B. Oral evaluation

Ask the participants to share the aspects of the workshop that were most valuable for them and for the improvement of their ministry. After the participants have had the opportunity to discuss the positive effects of the workshop, direct them to think of and share those aspects that need to be improved when repeating this experience with other people.

PART 3

Documents
and Resources

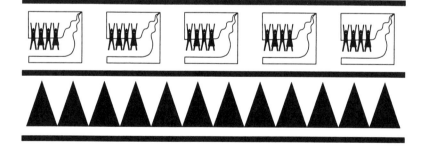

Prophets of Hope Process

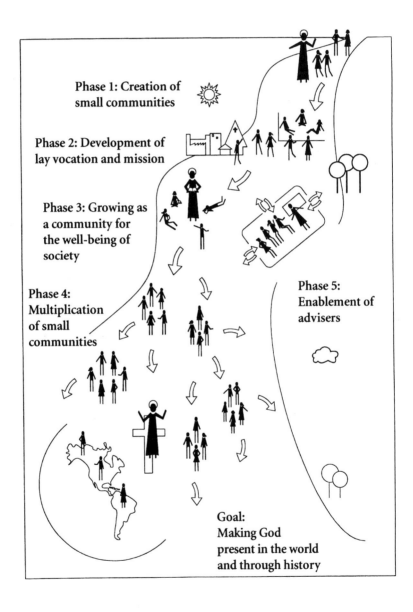

Phase 1: Creation of
small communities

Phase 2: Development of
lay vocation and mission

Phase 3: Growing as
a community for
the well-being of
society

Phase 4:
Multiplication
of small
communities

Phase 5:
Enablement of
advisers

Goal:
Making God
present in the world
and through history

The process of the Prophets of Hope model is made up of five related phases that encourage young Hispanics to live their Christian faith in the ecclesial, social, civic, and cultural spheres of society. These phases are:

Phase 1: Creation of small communities

The objectives of this phase are to establish one or more small communities in a particular location, and to initiate the participants into a communitarian type of reflection that will make them conscious of their evangelizing mission and motivate them to assume it.

Phase 2: Development of lay vocation and mission

The objective of this phase is to help the participants develop lay vocation and mission on the personal and community levels. This is accomplished in five stages that help them gradually fulfill their vision, formation, and commitment as Catholic Christians.

- Stage 1: Young people discover the presence of God in their life and listen to God's invitation to love one another and accept the salvation of Jesus.
- Stage 2: Young people come to know Jesus and interact with him as disciples—personally and in the community.
- Stage 3: Young people discern their vocation in life, study life's challenges, and become aware of their role in history.
- Stage 4: Young people come to know the church better, participate more actively in its sacramental and ministerial life, and begin their mission as lay evangelizers in the world.
- Stage 5: Young people undertake a lifelong project for themselves and the community that transforms them into agents of change in society.

Phase 3:
Growing as a community for the well-being of society

The objectives of this phase are: (a) to foster the growth and development of the small communities in such a way that the necessary conditions for a fulfilling communitarian experience are created; (b) to incarnate the communitarian experience in the lives of the participants, so that all they learn or live in the small community becomes an integral part of their daily life; and (c) to prepare leaders to create new communities and work with these communities in the initial stages.

Young people should decide, through a process of community discernment, when it is appropriate to enter this phase. Retreats that take place at the end of each formation phase help this discernment.

Phase 4: Multiplication of small communities

The objective of this phase is to build new small communities based on the experiences of those people who are already members of an established small community.

This phase may be repeated each year, or when people feel God is calling them to build a new community for a particular group of older adolescents or young adults. New communities also spring up from older communities that have grown too large for members to relate personally to one another and to participate fully in the group reflections. In these cases, each community should continue the process in which it was involved before splitting.

Phase 5: Enablement of advisers

The objective of this phase is to train people who want to be advisers for the small communities. It is important to keep in mind that the advisers are not members of the small communities, and, ideally, they are people who have been through the Prophets of Hope process.

Document 2

Roles in the Small Communities of *Jóvenes*

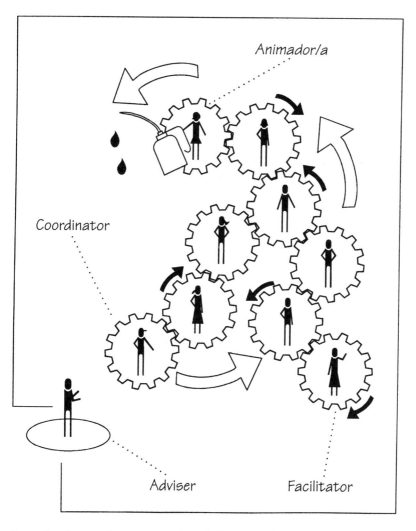

In order for small communities of *jóvenes* to become a seedbed for Christian leadership, all members must assume responsibility for the life of the community by learning to conduct meetings and other events. The Prophets of Hope model provides a variety of roles in each small community. Members also assume these roles or functions during events in which several communities are gathered. These include retreats, workshops, and days of reflection. Descriptions of the roles follow.

Animador/a

An *animador/a* is a member of the small community who motivates each member and the whole community, encourages all members to discover and develop their talents, and nurtures the life of the community *(animación)*. The role of an *animador/a* also includes the following:
• nurturing the prayer life of the community
• encouraging hospitality and mutual support among members
• supporting the community through difficult times

Animadores need to have certain charisms and adequate training. Communities choose an *animador/a* through a discernment process that helps them identify individuals who possess the needed gifts. In turn, the person chosen must discern whether God is calling him or her to render this service to the community at this particular time in life. An *animador/a* should not be chosen based on oral skills or the ability to organize and give orders, but on the personal qualities related to the functions stated above.

Extending beyond meetings, this function touches all aspects of community life. It is advisable for *animadores* to serve for a determined length of time—generally one year. At that time, the community undergoes the discernment process again to decide whether this member should continue as the *animador/a* or whether another person should be asked to serve.

Note: In this workshop it is not necessary to select an *animador/a* because of the short nature of the experience.

Coordinator

The coordinator is responsible for organizing and leading meetings and other community activities. She or he delegates different parts of the meeting or event to other members who serve as facilitator, timekeeper, or secretary.

Note: In this workshop it is not necessary to select a coordinator because of the short nature of the experience.

Facilitator

The facilitator is responsible for conducting a process for a specific part of the meeting and making sure all members participate in it. Principal duties include the following:
- encouraging members to participate in the process and interact with one another
- keeping the discussion focused on the theme
- leading the prayer

Timekeeper

The timekeeper makes sure that activities do not run over their allotted time.

Secretary

The secretary takes minutes of meetings. The principal duties are the following:
- writing down the main points made by each speaker, preserving the original train of thought
- reporting objectively what various members had to say or the conclusion reached by the group

Adviser

An adviser is a Christian who is mature in his or her faith, and is ready to serve *jóvenes* by sharing their life experiences and offering pastoral or professional advice. Advisers walk with *jóvenes* and counsel them on their faith journey. They are not regular members of the community, nor do they get directly involved in the community's activities. They are available to counsel and support the *animador/a* specifically and the community in general.

The Pastoral Circle
According to the Prophets of Hope Model

The Prophets of Hope model uses the pastoral circle as its methodological approach to foster a continuous Christian praxis process. This model recognizes young people's experience of life and promotes their human development and their life as a Christian community.

The pastoral circle takes into account the uniqueness of each person and community, and encourages youth and young adults to *be,* by accepting themselves for who they are and recognizing their dignity as sons and daughters of God. It helps young people to *see* the reality of their life and to *judge* that reality in light of the Gospel and the teachings of the church. It motivates young people to *act* and develop a Christian praxis, and to *evaluate* this praxis periodically to strengthen it.

The circle comes to an end and begins again with a celebration of life and faith. The *celebration* revitalizes and fortifies *jóvenes* and their communities to continue the pastoral circle with a familial spirit and Christian solidarity. The principal aspects fostered by the Prophets of Hope model, through the use of the pastoral circle, are the following:

Being

In the Prophets of Hope model, being refers to three dimensions of a person: being a unique and individual person; being a person in a continuous, developing process; and being a person in community. It also refers to being a community that is both evangelizing and missionary, and to being a community of communities, so that the small community looks at itself and acts in relation to other communities with an ecclesial spirit.

Seeing

The main reason for belonging to a *jóvenes* group or small community is to have a community of faith that assists us in building the Reign of God in society. For the Reign of God to take place, it is necessary to immerse oneself in everyday life and view reality from a Gospel perspective.

Seeing is becoming aware of the reality of life in five dimensions:

- the maturation process of the individual in relation to the psychology, the stages of development, the personality, the values, and the attitudes of the person
- the human relationships of *jóvenes* with their families, boyfriends or girlfriends, friends, neighbors, and peers from work or school
- the cultural situation of *jóvenes* in relation to the dominant culture in the United States, the culture of origin, the youth culture, and the modern and postmodern cultures
- the role of *jóvenes* in social transformation with its aspects related to work, the economy, education, and sociopolitical action

- the religious reality of *jóvenes*, including their beliefs, practices, spirituality, traditions, and education in the faith

Seeing reality in its five dimensions is accomplished by becoming aware of everyday occurrences, reflecting on key aspects of life, understanding the general environment, and undertaking a critical analysis of the systems and social structures that govern society. It is important to identify the following:

- the positive forces for human development, Christian growth, and pastoral action of *jóvenes*
- the pastoral needs that are generated from different aspects of life
- the challenges confronted by *jóvenes*
- the painful crosses that must be lived with a Christian spirit
- the causes behind the existence of the positive forces, pastoral needs, challenges, and crosses
- the contributions of the humanities and social sciences for an analysis of reality

Judging

As followers of Christ we need to see things from Jesus' perspective. We need to look at the ordinary and extraordinary events of life, the messages we get from others and the media, the sources of life and death in society, the opportunities for a better life, and the consequences of wrong decisions through the eyes of faith. Only then will we be able to discover God, encounter others who yearn for the new life offered by Jesus, recognize the dynamic between ourselves and reality, and respond better to God's call.

The Prophets of Hope model uses orientations and citations from the Scriptures and church documents to help *jóvenes* deepen their Christian faith, judge life according to Gospel criteria, discover God's call, and discern the way to respond to that call.

To judge in the light of faith, one must do the following:

- identify the reality or problem that one wants to judge
- question oneself on how Jesus would view this situation and how he would respond to it
- find in the Scriptures the necessary guidance to respond to the reality or problem
- investigate the position of the church's magisterium in relation to the problem or reality in question

- synthesize Jesus' and the church's perspective
- formulate, in a spirit of prayer, with a methodology of consensus, the pastoral-theological framework for the Christian praxis of the community

Acting

Being a disciple of Jesus means acting like Jesus. A faith without works is a dead faith. The mission of every Christian is to evangelize, announce the arrival of the Reign of God in the person of Jesus Christ, and prepare people to accept this gift of God. Fulfilling this mission means living a life inspired by the Gospel and working to make God's presence felt in the ordinary and extraordinary events of daily life.

The Prophets of Hope model encourages Christian actions on the part of small community members both individually and within the ecclesial community. The model does this through reflections that help members build the Reign of God in their immediate surroundings, evangelize their culture and society, and get involved in particular ministries according to their call.

Acting has to lead to the transformation or elimination of a situation that contradicts the Gospel. The two components of acting are the planning of an action or pastoral project, and its implementation. In the planning, one must diagnose the type of action that is necessary:

- action leading to creation, when the objective is to take an action or to develop a pastoral project from its beginning
- action leading to a transformation, when it is required to transform an existing situation based on an evaluation or critical analysis
- action leading to a solution, when the intent is to solve a problem, need, or conflict

Evaluating

Evaluating is key to improving the Christian praxis or the pastoral action of the small community by adjusting it to the new challenges presented by reality. Evaluation is done through ongoing discernment that helps participants become aware of their faith journey and of the need to continue their Christian life and formation. In addition, sessions are specifically designed for evaluating short periods of community life and Christian praxis. The evaluations serve to confirm or correct the praxis of the community. The three types of evaluation are as follows:

- continuous evaluation done at pre-established intervals throughout the planning process to make corrections and adjustments that ensure the success of the pastoral action
- final evaluation done after the specified period for the completion of an action or project to determine the type of pastoral impact the project has had on its participants and to identify those aspects of the project that can be improved
- mid- and long-term evaluation, done months or years after the implementation of the pastoral project has occurred, to determine the type of impact the project has had on the life and ministry of the participants

Celebrating

Being a prophet of hope requires the grace of God. To receive this gift, the prophet must have an open interior disposition acquired through prayer. God's gift will then lead the person to a joyful conversion and commitment to the mission of Jesus Christ.

In the Prophets of Hope model, faith celebrations are the peak experiences of the journeys, meetings, workshops, and retreats. These celebrations help participants experience the grace of God through personal and communal prayer, and provide them with a profound spiritual experience. During the regular community meetings, these celebrations are done in the small communities. During journeys, workshops, and retreats, these celebrations are done in the large community. In this way the community becomes both sign and instrument of personal conversion and community growth as *jóvenes* celebrate their commitment as disciples of Christ.

Celebrating sums up the pastoral experience during community gatherings and prayers. The three basic types of celebration are as follows:

- *Convivencias* and *fiestas* facilitate the expression of joy, and strengthen interpersonal relationships as a means of celebrating joined efforts in a completed project or pastoral action.
- Communitarian prayer occurs when the community gives thanks for their gifts, prays for forgiveness of human flaws, and calls out for God's help for the next stages of the pastoral action.

- The liturgy strengthens the spiritual life and the apostolic zeal of the participants, principally through the eucharistic celebration and liturgies of the word.

In summary, the pastoral circle helps us to *be* like Jesus, *see* reality from Jesus' perspective, *judge* reality on the basis of Jesus' Gospel and the teachings of the church, *act* to transform reality in ways similar to Jesus', *celebrate* to give thanks for God's gifts and to reinforce our faith to continue our Christian mission, and *evaluate* lifestyle and pastoral practices to improve the way of collaborating in Jesus' mission.

Witnesses of Hope Collection

Series	Titles	Objectives	Phases of the Process
Prophets of Hope	Volume 1 *Hispanic Young People and the Church's Pastoral Response*	Analyzes the personal, social, cultural, and religious reality of Hispanic *jóvenes*, and the response of the church to their pastoral needs	Enablement of *animadores* and advisers
	Volume 2 *Evangelization of Hispanic Young People*	Focuses on the evangelization of Hispanic *jóvenes*, the model of evangelization used in small communities, and the role of Mary in evangelization	
	Volume 3 *The Prophets of Hope Model: A Weekend Workshop*	Offers a process for experiencing the Prophets of Hope model and learning its pastoral-theological foundations	Initial experience of the Prophets of Hope model
Agents of Hope	Manual 1 *Dawn on the Horizon: Creating Small Communities*	Aids in the creation of small communities through a formation-in-action process lived and facilitated by people sixteen to twenty-four years of age	Creation and multiplication of small communities
	Manual 2 *Leaven in the World: Growing in Community Life*	Helps the participants appreciate the meaning of community life and enables them to take responsibility for their own communities	Growing as a community for the well-being of society
	Manual 3 *Servants of the Reign of God: Advising Small Communities*	Helps train adults as advisers of small communities through an active formation process and pastoral practice	Enablement of advisers

Series	Titles	Objectives	Phases of the Process
Builders of Hope	Book 1 *In Covenant with God*	Fosters the vocation and mission of the members of the community in the history of salvation from a theological and anthropological perspective	
	Book 2 *Followers of Jesus*	Fosters the vocation and mission of the members of the community as disciples from a christological perspective	
	Book 3 *Acting Through History*	Fosters the vocation and mission of the members of the community in their immediate environments from a social perspective	Development of lay vocation and mission
	Book 4 *Committed as Church*	Fosters the vocation and mission of the members of the community from an ecclesial perspective	
	Book 5 *Fostering Culture and Society*	Fosters the vocation and mission of the members of the community from a sociocultural perspective	

Personal Gifts for Serving the Community

It is important for us to recognize our areas of strength and those areas we need to work on and develop. For each of the following qualities, gifts, and charisms, rate the level you have attained, using a 1 to 5 scale. A 5 means you have attained the highest possible level in that attribute. For example, if you can sing extremely well, put a 5; if you can sing well, put a 4; if your singing is average, put a 3; if this area is weak, put a 1 or a 2. When you finish, add up all your points.

Gifts   **Score from 1 to 5**

1. I can sing or play music.   _____
2. I welcome and accept others.   _____
3. I take time for personal prayer.   _____
4. I am informed about what goes on in the world.   _____
5. I am willing to serve.   _____
6. I work with enthusiasm and zeal.   _____
7. I am an optimist.   _____
8. I am concerned about my faith formation.   _____
9. I have a good sense of humor.   _____
10. I cultivate friendship.   _____
11. I am honest.   _____
12. I motivate and affirm others.   _____
13. I know how to take notes in meetings.   _____
14. I know how to listen to others.   _____
15. I help resolve conflicts.   _____
16. I can coordinate a meeting.   _____
17. I am responsible.   _____
18. I can both lead and follow.   _____
19. I work well in a team.   _____
20. I communicate well.   _____

Total: _____

Reflections on the Five Dimensions of Reality

Jóvenes and their process of maturation

In their process of maturation, the participants should aim to do at
least one of the following:
- achieve the harmonious integration of their identity and their personality
- promote the development and utilization of their personal talents
- facilitate a continuous process of conversion and faith formation,
  focused on a willingness to serve others
- create space and appropriate opportunities so that they may express their feelings, articulate their experiences, and share their
  creativity
- keep the hope alive, fostering their human growth in times of crisis, during conflict, and in the struggle against the challenges of life

    1. Other important factors not mentioned in this list are . . .

    2. The gifts and qualities that the *jóvenes* have in the process of
maturation are . . .

    3. The challenges
faced by the *jóvenes* in
the process of maturation are . . .

Interpersonal relations of *jóvenes*

When one speaks about the interpersonal relations of *jóvenes*, it is important to take several factors, such as the following, into account:
- the Hispanic communitarian spirit
- the relationship between the *jóven* and his or her family, the Latino concept of family, and the various types of families young people belong to
- friendship among *jóvenes*
- the perspective from which *jóvenes* deal with human sexuality, the relationship between the sexes, and the impact of society on attitudes toward sexuality
- the stance and behavior of *jóvenes* in relation to dating and marriage

1. Other important factors not mentioned in this list are . . .

2. The gifts and qualities that the *jóvenes* have in the area of interpersonal relations are . . .

3. The challenges faced by the *jóvenes* in the area of interpersonal relations are . . .

The role of *jóvenes* in social transformation

Jóvenes play an important role in the present and the future of a country. Their influence is felt in the economic, political, social, and cultural realms. They exert a positive influence when they promote a society without prejudice, when they work for justice and peace, and when they participate productively in the society. Four areas for transformation of today's society are family life, the mass media, ecology, and politics.

1. Other important factors not mentioned in this paragraph are . . .

2. The gifts and qualities that the *jóvenes* have in regard to social transformation are . . .

3. The challenges faced by the *jóvenes* in regard to social transformation are . . .

The religious life of *jóvenes*

The religious reality of *jóvenes* is complex. It includes aspects of *religiosidad popular*—expressing their faith and reinforcing their cultural identity—and a unique way of living a Catholicism, whose roots lie in Latin America, in the United States. But the most important factors in the religious reality of *jóvenes* are the way they live their Christian faith, their level of evangelization and commitment to Jesus Christ, and their response from a personal faith perspective to the challenges brought by the society and the culture where they live.

1. Other important factors not mentioned in this paragraph are . . .

2. The gifts and qualities that the *jóvenes* have in regard to religious life are . . .

3. The challenges faced by the *jóvenes* in regard to religious life are . . .

Cultural context of *jóvenes*

Human beings live, grow, and develop in a cultural context. In the culture and through it, people establish their roots, grow, nourish their customs and values, and journey toward maturity. Simultaneously, *jóvenes* are being influenced by culture and are creating their own culture. This culture has distinct levels of depth, which include the following:

- an exterior level made up of objects, fashion, and technology used
- a second level consisting of language, art, tradition, and customs, through which a people relates and expresses its existence
- a third level made up of the systems and social institutions where life unfolds and that a people uses to transmit its culture
- a fourth level where values that give meaning to life are rooted
- a fifth level where the meaning and purpose of life is found

1. Other important factors not mentioned in this list are . . .

2. The gifts and qualities that the *jóvenes* have in regard to cultural context are . . .

3. The challenges faced by the *jóvenes* in regard to cultural context are . . .

Themes for a Reflection on Christian Faith and Life

Reflection on my Covenant with God

Using the texts and questions presented below, reflect on your Covenant with God, that is, the way you see God's presence in your life, the way you feel God's love toward you, and the way you share that love with others.

> Now may the God of peace, who brought back from the dead our Lord Jesus, the great shepherd of the sheep, by the blood of the eternal covenant, make you complete in everything good so that you may do his will, working among us that which is pleasing in his sight, through Jesus Christ, to whom be the glory forever and ever. Amen. (Hebrews 13:20–21)

> We believe in God the Father, good and generous, who has called us and guided us up to this point. . . . We believe in Jesus Christ, our Lord and Savior, revealed in our history through his loving and transforming presence. . . . We believe in the Holy Spirit, in the inspiration and strength given by [the Holy Spirit] to our leaders, and in the love, light, and unity . . . brought forth among all those gathered here. (Secretariat for Hispanic Affairs, *Prophetic Voices*, p. 17)

1. In what ways do you live your Covenant of love with God and with other people?

2. How would you like to improve the way you live this Covenant?

Reflection on my following of Jesus

Using the texts and questions presented below, reflect on your following of Jesus, that is, the way you relate with Jesus, follow him as one of his disciples, and learn from him how to live.

"I give you a new commandment, that you love one another. Just as I have loved you, you also should love one another. By this everyone will know that you are my disciples, if you have love for one another." (John 13:34–35)

We believe in our identification with Christ, as the suffering people we are. We believe, even as he did, in the divinity of all human beings and in their liberation through love. For this reason, we support and collaborate in the struggle of the poor, who have been humiliated and marginalized, in this way building the Kingdom among us, until all attain everlasting beatitude. (Secretariat for Hispanic Affairs, *Prophetic Voices,* p. 17)

1. In what ways do you live your discipleship with Jesus?

2. How would you like to improve the way you live your discipleship?

Reflection on my role in history

Using the texts and questions presented below, reflect on your role in history, that is,
how Jesus' Gospel can inspire you to transform your life through your interaction with
family, friends, work, and school.

> What good is it, my brothers and sisters, if you say you have
> faith but do not have works? Can faith save you? If a brother or
> sister is naked and lacks daily food, and one of you says to them,
> "Go in peace; keep warm and eat your fill," and yet you do not
> supply their bodily needs, what is the good of that? So faith by
> itself, if it has no works, is dead. (James 2:14–17)

> We believe that serving others is the best manner of evangeliz-
> ing and that we are doing this by our actions, for we are sowers
> of the Word, springs of faith, tireless searchers of the light, in-
> struments of healing and reconciliation, and a prophetic voice
> for the present, as well as the sign of a new dawn in the mosaic
> of the Catholic Church in the United States. (Secretariat for
> Hispanic Affairs, *Prophetic Voices*, p. 18)

1. What do you do in your everyday life to contribute to everyone's history being a history of salvation?

2. How would you like to improve the way you act in your
everyday life?

Reflection on my mission and my commitment to the church

Using the texts and questions presented below, reflect on your mission and commitment to the church, that is, the way you participate in the ecclesial community and bring Jesus' Gospel to others.

> They devoted themselves to the apostles' teaching and fellowship, to the breaking of bread and the prayers. Awe came upon everyone, because many wonders and signs were being done by the apostles. All who believed were together and had all things in common. (Acts 2:42–44)

> The Church's mission is three-fold: to proclaim the good news of salvation; to offer itself as a group of people transformed by the Spirit into a community of faith, hope, and love; and to bring God's justice and love to others through service in its individual, social and political dimensions. (USCC, *A Vision of Youth Ministry*, p. 3)

1. In what ways do you participate in the ecclesial community and bring Jesus' Gospel to others?

2. How would you like to improve your participation in the church and the way you fulfill your evangelizing mission?

Reflection on my role
in building culture and society

Using the texts and questions presented below, reflect on your role in building culture and society, that is, the way you foster a culture and a society inspired by Jesus Christ.

> For the creation waits with eager longing for the revealing of the children of God; for the creation was subjected to futility, not of its own will but by the will of the one who subjected it, in hope that the creation itself will be set free from its bondage to decay and will obtain the freedom of the glory of the children of God. (Romans 8:19–21)

> It is our personal witness through action that will dramatically offer hope to a world that seems hopeless. (Secretariat for Hispanic Affairs, *Proceedings of the II Encuentro Nacional Hispano de Pastoral,* p. 56)

1. In what ways do you fulfill your mission of being a builder of culture and society?

2. How would you like to improve the way you undertake this mission?

Praxis of a Community of Disciples of Jesus

The goal of small ecclesial communities lies in facilitating their members' commitment to living out the Gospel and, with the same spirit as the first Christian communities, carrying the Good News to others. This commitment to discipleship and Christian action, when done in a critical manner in light of the Gospel, is called Christian praxis, or community praxis. To achieve this goal, small communities try to maintain a balance between different practices appropriate to a community of Jesus' disciples. Together these practices—carried out every day, not just on the days the small group meets—constitutes the life of a true small ecclesial community.

Certainly not all small communities follow the same pattern: each chooses the element or elements that it wishes to emphasize, according to its members' vocations and needs. Some small communities emphasize prayer, missionary evangelization, Bible study, or faith reflection. Others revolve around members' ministry, the need for a support group, or desire for Christian formation for action.

To become more aware of the experience of your group or community, and of those areas where you need to work harder to become a more authentic Christian community, each participant should prioritize the following practices, placing first the one he or she needs to work on the most:

- **sharing life,** with its ups and downs, sadness and joy, failures and successes, in such a way that the members of the community accept, care for, and love one another as sons and daughters of God
- **sharing prayer,** with both spontaneous and structured prayers of petition, thanksgiving, praise, and forgiveness, all leading to the culminating act of thanksgiving—the celebration of the Eucharist
- **sharing faith,** reflecting together on the Scriptures, and mutually edifying one another by retelling experiences of God's action in their personal life and among the people of faith
- **evangelizing and serving others,** not only within the community but, above all, beyond it: bearing witness to Christian life in all settings of daily life and engaging in concrete missionary efforts to carry Jesus to persons who have not found him or have moved away from his love

- **deepening in faith** through study of the Scriptures and church teachings relating faith to life; trying to discover God's presence or absence in the social, economic, cultural, and political worlds; striving to identify the signs of the times through which God calls the community members to personal conversion and to transform the world so that love, justice, and peace might reign

The scriptural quotations in this book are from the New Revised Standard Version of the Bible. Copyright © 1989 by the Division of Christian Education of the National Council of the Churches of Christ in the United States. All rights reserved.

The excerpt on page 9 is from the *National Pastoral Plan for Hispanic Ministry* (Washington, DC: United States Catholic Conference [USCC], 1988), page 8. Copyright © 1988 by the USCC, Washington, DC 20017. All rights reserved.

The excerpts on pages 60, 61, and 62 are from *Prophetic Voices: The Document on the Process of the III Encuentro Nacional Hispano de Pastoral* (Washington, DC: USCC, 1986), pages 17–18. Copyright © 1986 by the USCC, Washington, DC 20017. A related publication, *Hispanic Ministry: Three Major Documents,* can be obtained by calling USCC Publishing Services 800-235-8722. Used with permission. All rights reserved.

The excerpt on page 63 is from *A Vision of Youth Ministry* (Washington, DC: USCC, 1986), page 3. Copyright © 1986 by the USCC, Washington, DC 20017. All rights reserved.

The excerpt on page 64 is from *Proceedings of the II Encuentro Nacional Hispano de Pastoral* (Washington, DC: USCC, 1978), page 56. Copyright © 1978 by the USCC, Washington, DC 20017. All rights reserved.

 NOTES

NOTES

 NOTES

 NOTES

NOTES